Shades of Lakeland

A collection of watercolour paintings
and descriptions of favourite Lakeland walks

by

Kathleen Gilbert

Kathleen Gilbert

PUBLISHED BY GLARAMARA STUDIOS

FIRST EDITION 2002

ISBN 978 0-9543491-0-5

During her working life Kathleen took delight in imparting a love of Art and English to children from the ages of nine to sixteen and eventually became Headteacher of Throckley Middle School on the outskirts of Newcastle upon Tyne. She has always loved poetry and art but it is only since her retirement that she has been able to indulge her passion for pen and brush. Widely travelled, Kathleen experiments with a variety of subjects and styles but her great love is in the landscapes of the Lake District where she and her husband are frequent visitors.

Kathleen has had solo exhibitions in Newcastle and Keswick.

Introduction

Sometimes when I am away from the Lake District I try to imprint on my memory some of the walks I have enjoyed. I rehearse pictures in my mind's eye so that they may be conjured up more easily in those quiet times at home; moments of delight which, as Wordsworth said in his best known poem, 'flash upon that inward eye which is the bliss of solitude'. Believing these images may be of significance to others, I have tried to capture them in words, paintings and sketches, hoping that they might rekindle enduring memories for you.

CONTENTS

Continued..........

Contents continued:-

A

TRANQUIL CIRCUMNAVIGATION

ON A

LAKESHORE PATH

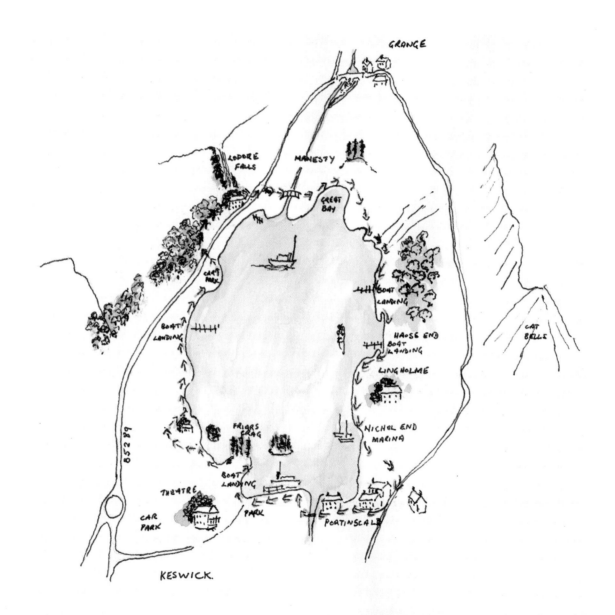

GRANGE

LODORE FALLS

MANESTY

GREAT BAY

CAR PARK

BOAT LANDING

BOAT LANDING

HAUSE END BOAT LANDING

CAT BELLS

LINGHOLME

FRIARS CRAG

NICHOL END MARINA

B 5289

THEATRE

BOAT LANDING

CAR PARK

PARK

PORTINSCALE

KESWICK.

8

A TRANQUIL CIRCUMNAVIGATION ON A LAKESHORE PATH

The joys which Derwentwater's shores hold for the walker are unparalleled, transcending seasons and weather. They are to be treasured like jewels in the secret compartments of memory, taken out in quiet moments, polished with love and hidden away in the knowledge that they are always there to bring delight to some drab corner of existence.

A circuit of the lake may be made in either direction and may be shortened by using the lake steamer. If you are travelling by car, park in one of the many parking areas in Keswick or in the Lakeside car park and head down to the steamer landing on the lake. It is a good idea to collect a timetable, so that you know where and when you will be able to catch a return steamer. There is a service all year round except Christmas Day, but from December to February it is very limited. You may wish to cross the lake to Hawse End and commence the circuit from there. These directions are from Keswick.

During a severe winter, you may be fortunate enough to see the lake near the landings, completely frozen and safe enough for skaters to venture far out onto the ice, just and they did in Wordsworth's time. On other days, black water slaps the sides of boats moored at the landing stages and they groan and creak in reply. Ducks crouch down amongst the pebbles, looking hopefully at passers by. Across the lake, the ridge of Causey Pike wriggles like Nessy, dark against the skyline leading up to a high ridge walk over Sail and Eel Crags.

Turning left, you may choose to walk along the shingled shore or on a higher level tar-macadamed path past the boat jetties, heading through trees beside the lake. When the tarmac peters out, a popular and well worn track continues, a favourite stroll for many locals and visitors to the Lake District. This is not surprising for its destination is Friar's Crag, a rocky promontory overlooking the length of Derwentwater. Views from here are spectacular. In the distance, line of lake and fell converge on the jagged blue silhouette of Castle Crag.

(Continued on page 11)

The boat landing at Keswick is the start of our exploration of Derwentwater. Boats moored here creak and groan with the constant movement of water. Ducks forage on the shingle. This is one of many bays worn into the shores of Derwentwater all of which have a distinctive character and hold visual interest for the walker.

Derwentwater

Derwentwater - misty, blue ,ethereal.
Picturesque at all times
And in all seasons.
A walk along its shore
Reveals many bays,
Some inhabited by boats,
Others by birds.

Peaceful sounds of lake water turning on a pebbled shore, and the soughing of a gentle breeze in pine trees are balm to those who bring with them the stress of everyday living. This is nature's antidote and better by far than Valium or other prescribed medications. An inscription on a memorial to John Ruskin states that, 'the spirit of God is all around you,' and who could dispute that sentiment. A tiny bay, perfectly scooped out, lies beneath the crag. This is a favourite haunt of greylag geese who honk and gossip, break ranks and reform as though they were out on a W.I. day trip. Fallen pine trunks and seats in splendid locations make this a place to tarry and take in the scene but this is a lengthy walk with many beautiful spots, so try to limit your stay.

The path now leads through reeds and meadows into woodland. In summer, the scent of Sweet Cecily pervades the air and there are wild raspberries to be sampled. Pass through a gate and turn right along a metalled path which curves round a meadow and passes Stable Hills Cottage. The lake reappears and the path rises to a promontory which affords wonderful views of Causey Pike and Derwentwater. Continue through fir trees and down to the waters edge. Here, you will find an interesting slate sculpture like a split egg with smoothed and patterned surfaces. A noisy clamour of pink footed geese may pervade the air as they gather in Calf Close Bay. The ground is carpeted with dried twigs over scoured shingle. Exposed roots of trees appear as polished silver. Ahead, there is a stately stand of pine trees. Walk on the pebbled shore or path, whichever you choose. Here there may be the drone of a passing steamer and the sound of ripples from its wake busily caressing the stony shore. Across the lake, the gracefully curving fell like a reclining figure with an amply rounded hip, is Cat Bells and Hawse End. It is believed that the name Cat Bells has been derived from the words Cat Bield home of the wild cat. The crag above you is Walla Crag, a place which presents splendid views of Derwentwater and the surrounding fells. On a strip of shingle beside the road leading up to Ashness Bridge you will find a ferry landing.

Continue along the shore, crossing a stile and a bridge. Here the grass is cropped short by sheep and there are beautiful open views of the lake; Skiddaw, patterned by passing clouds in one direction and Castle Crag in the other. Cross over a stile onto a shingled terrace which leads to Kettlewell car park. There is always something going on here. There may be a party of canoeists about to launch their craft onto the blue waters. Their bright

(Continued over)

red and yellow life jackets and hulls of their craft, contrast strongly with the cool colours around them. Mallard waddle out onto the pebbles, hoping that the odd crust might be thrown in their direction. Chaffinches, tame enough to eat from the hand, busy themselves picking up crumbs which have fallen amongst stones. As a steamer passes, its wake sends still reflections dancing and fragmenting, its undertow dragging at the pebbled shore. Sequins of sunlight sparkle, enlivening the tops of wavelets and setting the lake surface a-shimmer. A place of peaceful activity to be enjoyed by all.

Now turn your back on the lake, leave the car park and cross over the main road with care. Go through a gap in the wall opposite onto a path through the woods continuing parallel with the road. Here steep cliffs rise above you and in summer there is the smell of garlic. If you're observant you may see a shy wren skulking in the bracken or hear its harsh chirring alarm call. Pass the Mary Mount Hotel and follow the path away from the road. Trees are wound round with ivy stems, linking and holding like a sculpture of two lovers.

Soon you will hear the sound of the Lodore Falls and you will see a finger post pointing in their direction. Make your way round the back of the Lodore Hotel and return to the road. If you wish to shorten your walk, there is another ferry landing opposite the Lodore, otherwise walk along the road for a short while. There are public toilets diagonally opposite the Lodore Hotel. Soon you will see a finger post pointing across the fields signposted 'public Footpath to Manesty'. Take this path as it threads its way through reeds and water meadows towards a bridge arched like those depicted on willow pattern plates. After rain, this area can be very wet and I have seen it totally flooded, the bridge standing amidst a sheet of water and the footpath sign, 'To Manesty' inviting a miracle of walking on water to achieve that goal. Braided locks, white waterfalls, fly in wayward winds, appearing in every crack and gully. Trees stand oxter deep in raging rivers and grey lakes become sheets of billowing silk.

(Continued on page 14)

Skiddaw, 3,053 feet, is the fourth highest peak in the Lake District. Seen here from Manesty, it makes an impressive backdrop to Derwentwater. In summer months, there are often sunsets which turn sky and lake to blood red.

On dry days, the path leads on, through clouds of purple grasses which turn ochre in Autumn and bend to a stiff breeze. In Spring, blue rivulets are bordered by yellow celandines. Above is the graceful outline of Skiddaw, sometimes navy blue and threatening, sometimes patterned purple and bronze, homely and welcoming. On summer evenings, this scene can be turned blood red as the sun dips down behind the fells. Beneath the bridge run clear waters as the River Derwent makes its way towards the lake. Now the path is raised above the marshy land on wooden walkways. These can become very slippery when wet. The walkway leads to some delightful craggy knolls and bays always graced by Skiddaw on the skyline. In July, purple and yellow orchids grow in wet land beneath the walkway. Soon a glimpse of Blencathra appears across the lake and Walla Crag juts out from its skirt of trees and bracken. Beneath its frown lies the Lodore Hotel.

Eventually the path goes through a gate into beech woodland always close to the lake. Enjoy the green stillness of a bay paved with glossy lily pads. In July, cream, waxy blossoms are reflected in its dark waters.

When you come to a row of cottages on a metalled track, turn right and head for Abbot's Bay. Pass through a kissing gate in front of Brandlehow cottage, down to the shore and over a stile. Here shaley banks rise steeply to the road along the west shore. At the water's edge, there are many smooth, flat stones crying out to be used for skimming the lake surface in duck and drakes. A wash from a passing steamer sweeps the pebbles, shredding reflections into ribbons of cerulean silk. Stillness and silence follow.

Round the corner, beyond the bay is High Brandlehow landing stage surrounded by picnic tables. There are splendid views of Blencathra and of a promontory with a secluded white house set amongst dark trees. Tufted duck and pochard sometimes drift to and fro just off shore. The path now enters Brandlehow Park, winding through fine beech, oak and fir trees. This is an area of exquisite woodland where redwoods stand in simple dignity amidst cathedral calm. Here, the lakeshore is beautiful in all seasons but colours in Autumn, reflected in the lake's still waters are particularly stunning. Amongst the Scots pine coal tits indulge in acrobatics,

(Continued on page 16)

A tranquil moment may be enjoyed in one of the many picturesque picnic spots on the shores of Derwentwater.

seeking out seeds from fir cones and swinging upside down, moving from twig to twig. Tree creepers jerkily move round the girth, exploring cracks in the bark for tiny insects. The path winds through trees or, if you wish, you may walk along the pebbled shore. Pause for a paddle to cool tired feet and enjoy the changing vistas and patterns of mottled sunlight on moving water.

Low Brandlehow landing stage comes into view. Pass through the gate in the wall and keep to the path bordering the lake, ignoring the left turn. Over a rocky promontory, drop down towards a reed filled bay. Here the path briefly leaves the lake. Follow it around a fenced area and when it rejoins the broader path, turn right. Bear right at the next fork, returning to the lake through woodland where there are musky scents of rotting foliage and damp wood. Horse chestnut trees hold out their leaves like fingers from great palms turned up to capture Autumn sunshine. This is a place to wander, enjoying the peace and tranquillity, a space which is your own to lock into memory. Soon you will arrive at the landing stage at Hawse End. This is a good place to end your walk and take the steamer back to Keswick. Make sure that it is the boat travelling clockwise or else you will retrace your steps in a watery fashion. If you really want to claim a true circumnavigation, it is possible to continue by heading up though the woods, turning right to head for Lingholme Gardens. The path eventually leads to Nichol End Marina where there is another landing stage and the possibility of cups of tea and toilets. From here, the way is mainly by road, through Portinscale, passing the Derwentwater Hotel and following the field path to Keswick.

You have circumnavigated Derwentwater, the Queen of Lakes, and stored images to cherish in absentia.

Brandelhow

Autumn days in Brandelhow
Bring paths carpeted with leaves
Ginger as a fox's coat.
Still waters turn idly onto pebbled shores
And trees are mirrored
On their silvered surface.

TO AN ANCIENT HAMLET

AND

THROUGH THE JAWS OF BORROWDALE

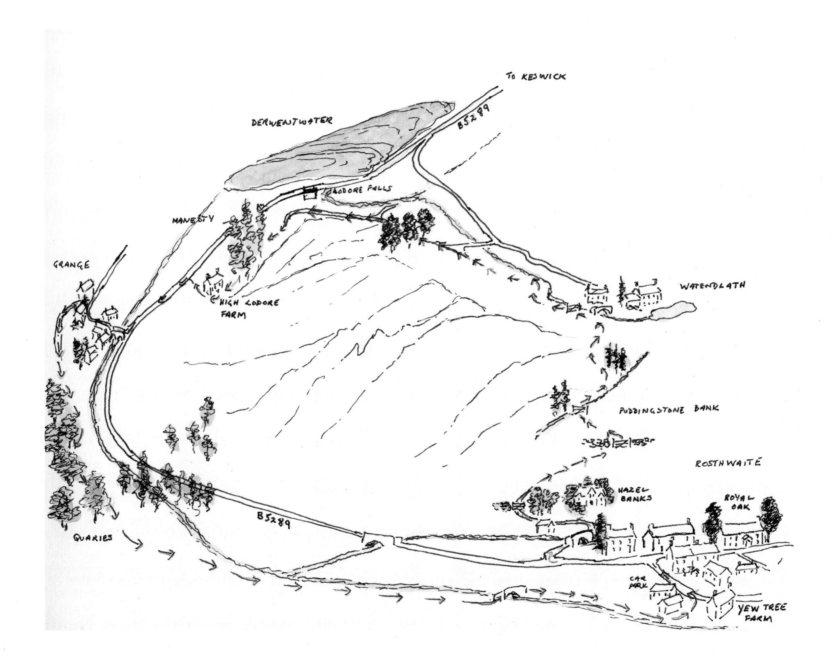

TO KESWICK

DERWENTWATER

B5289

LODORE FALLS

MANESTY

GRANGE

HIGH LODORE FARM

WATENDLATH

PUDDINGSTONE BANK

ROSTHWAITE

HAZEL BANKS

ROYAL OAK

QUARIES

B5289

CAR PARK

YEW TREE FARM

18

TO AN ANCIENT HAMLET AND THROUGH THE JAWS OF BORROWDALE

Following the old bridle way across the fells from Rosthwaite to Watendlath is full of delights to savour from small secrets to cinemascopic panoramas and is a favourite pilgrimage of all who stay in Borrowdale.

Approaching Rosthwaite from Keswick, a lane just before the village leads to Hazel Bank. This is the start of a bridle way which, in the not so distant past, was Borrowdale's direct route to the Vale of St. John and Grasmere.

Pause on the bridge to look over the parapet at the River Derwent chattering on green slate and muse at the water level marker. After severe rain or snow melt the river has been known to rise rapidly, breaking its banks, flooding the back bar at the Scafell Hotel and the ground floor of the Royal Oak. On the other side of the valley, a groove winds through the deserted waste of Rigg Head Quarries and on to Dale Head.

Bear left after the bridge, pass the camping barn and as the track begins to climb, enjoy views down the valley towards Derwentwater. Two larch trees are prominent in the landscape standing close together courting and dancing in sudden gusts of breeze. Here a raised footpath keeps feet dry in wet weather, leading on through dappled sunlight and shade, towards a gate. Tumbling streams probe ways beneath trees, through walls and over stones, hurrying down to meet the Derwent. Bear right at the gate and climb up the great brown shoulder of earth towards a gate in a wall. Now the track bears left up the fell side. Above the wall is the knobbly line of Joppelty How what a wonderful name and King's How. In Autumn, the fells here seem like burnished copper as bracken glows with rich browns and golds. At this point, if you are still and listen carefully, you may hear the laugh of a green woodpecker from the trees on the left. Another gate on the brow of a rise is a good place to rest and let the eye trace tracks up distant fells. Rosthwaite Fell, Glaramara, Seathwaite Fell, all crouch like hounds waiting for their master's call. At their feet, diminished to the size of toys, lie the white cottages of Rosthwaite. In the early morning, mists lend the view an ethereal quality and a peacefulness which lingers in the memory.

Beside the gate, tall pine trees shade glinting water as it glosses over stones, enlivening bracken banks with sound and movement. The path crosses the stream and climbs upwards over smoothed boulders to the crest of the ridge. Soon the view opens up before us towards Armboth Fell, ripped apart by great gashes worn by ancient water courses. Below lies Watendlath Tarn, dark as a pansy's petal, and the cluster of houses which make up this lonely hamlet. All seems quiet, deserted almost and ears and eyes strain for sights and sounds of habitation, the bark of a dog perhaps or drone of a tractor. Then as we descend and the image becomes reality, we notice washing on the line, farmers working with their sheep in the fold, cows in the barn and the road from Keswick which brings droves of tourists during the summer season. Far better to approach Watendlath over the fells as we have done.

If you're ready for a picnic, often a good place to sit is in the shelter of the wall near the tarn. However, be prepared to share your sandwiches with the locals - chaffinches here are greedy and quite tame and the cross bred ducks verge on being aggressive. I don't think you could escape without allowing them to have just a few crumbs!

A picturesque bridge crosses the water outlet from the tarn. Take time to notice the wonderful ferns clinging to crevices in the dry stone wall of the bridge and look for the slab in the paving at the entrance to the bridge marked '22.5.95 H.R.H. Prince Charles' Look out over the tarn and marvel at the effects of changing light on water.

To proceed, do not cross the bridge into the village but follow the path along by the beck which tumbles over grey boulders and then between sliced rocks, creating delightful cascades. The path now winds around by the stream until it straightens out on the more level ground of the valley floor. Here, where water rushes and

(Continued on page 22)

Borrowdale

Time after time we return to Borrowdale
And greet the hills as old friends.
Gradually each hill becomes known to us
Not only by name but by the tread of our boots.
Each return is a new experience,
The hills are the same, eternally present,
But their garments change continually
With the seasons and the climate;
Golden bracken...ice...snow...rain...mist...sunshine

Kathleen Gilbert

If you are a lover of wildlife, sitting in the shelter of a wall at the edge of Watendlath Tarn is a pleasant experience. Birds of all varieties come to share your packed lunch. If you are not willing to share, then while you are admiring the view they will steal your sandwiches. The tarn is stocked with trout and perch and there are usually fishermen trying out their skills. The unusual name Watendlath, is believed to be derived from the Scandinavian word vatn which means lake.

bubbles in a friendly commotion, is a good place to look out for dippers, plump brown and white birds which bob up and down on boulders and dive below the surface of these miniature torrents. Rock pinnacles rise on the left, a haunt of buzzards.

Now the path divides. Ignore the way signposted for Keswick and head up through the trees to the left.
When a river comes into view, bear left along a narrow path (the main track continues down to the river past a seat) cross over a stile and at this point, the start of the cataract comes into view. Turn left along its banks and enjoy the power of this water as it surges below. This is the start of the famous Lodore Falls. At this point there are many picturesque places for picnics.

Just as the path starts to swing left again and the water heads off towards its plunge over the rock face, it is possible to catch a glimpse of Derwentwater and Skiddaw through the autumn and winter trees, a secret and private view above Lodore. Beside the water the ground rises to the head of Shepherd's Crag, a favourite nursery pitch for would-be rock climbers. Listen for the sound of their voices or the metallic echo of pitons in the still air.

Our way starts to descend, at first through bracken and then through woodland. Below lie the fields of Manesty and beyond, the crags of Maiden Moor. Ignoring tracks branching off to the right, head down towards the road. Walk through High Lodore Farm, where in season you may be able to enjoy a welcome cup of tea and piece of cake and turn left, crossing the busy Keswick road with care, heading for Grange. Once past the Borrowdale Hotel, look for a gap in the wall on the right, which will take you onto a path away from the road. In Autumn, pause on the graceful double arched bridge to admire the brilliant gold and copper tones reflected in the green water of the river Derwent. Sometimes the crags above are sprinkled with early snows, a perfect foil for the warmth of autumn colours.

Grange is a good place to stop for tea and scones, a bowl of soup, and toilets, then the path leads on beside the café with the veranda, through delightful woodland, towards Rosthwaite. At first, whenever you have a choice,

(Continued on page 23)

Watendlath

In weak winter sunlight,
The grey silk of Watendlath Tarn shimmers,
Its watermarks circling worn rocks.
A bridge arches its back over a beck
Rouched and frilled like a cavalier's cravat.
Farmsteads wait, their windows watching the skyline
As for some long expected homecoming.
Watendlath - other worldly, wistfully waiting,
A solitary place, lost in its timeless valley.

Grange

Sudden October snowfall
Etches the bones of fells.
Burnished golds of Autumn
Glow on the surface of jade pools.
Beneath the shadow
Of a twin arched bridge,
Derwent's waters flow slowly on
Chilled to its stony bed.
Blue wood smoke wreathes upwards
From white cottages held
In counterpoint by dark conifers.
All has been called
To a rehearsal of Winter's cold embrace.

take the left hand fork until you arrive at a wonderful sweep of the river with wide gravelly shores. Here you might be fortunate enough to see a goosander, a large sawbill duck with white breast and green head, revelling in the swift currents. When you are ready, continue on the path beside the river crossing two bridges. After the second bridge DO NOT TURN RIGHT go straight ahead to a gate at the top of a rise. Through the gate there is a seat overlooking the river. You are now beside one of the loveliest stretches of the Derwent. Its waters here are usually still and jade green. They hold perfect reflections of trees reaching upwards to patches of sky. The path threads its way up and around and through trees, over crags beside the river, leading you through the jaws of Borrowdale.

At a level clearing it turns sharp right heading away from the river and eventually uphill. If you miss this turning you will find yourself at a sloping slab which blocks the path and slopes right down to the water. It is possible to scramble over it, but safer to retrace your steps to find the correct path. Ignore the gap in the wall where a stream has made its way and continue to the next opening which will lead through the old quarry spoil heaps beneath the glowering rocks of Castle Crag.

Presently our way leaves the woodland and rejoins the river in open pasture. Now the view opens up over fields sloping down from High Spy, Rigg Head Quarries and Castle Crag. There are high tracks including an old mine road which leads from Grange to Honister which you might like to explore on another occasion. Soon you will come to a slate bridge over the Derwent and a track which leads you through Yew Tree Farm and back to Rosthwaite. You have completed a circuit of one of the loveliest areas of the Lake District to an Ancient Hamlet and through the Jaws of Borrowdale.

The path from Grange to Rosthwaite passes through one of the loveliest areas in the Lake District, the Jaws of Borrowdale. Here, the River Derwent appears to be jade green as it flows over its bed of Borrowdale slate.

Rosthwaite

Rosthwaite's humble huddle of houses
Holds a quiet charm.
A comfortable marriage of green slate
Mossy stones and white walls.
An ancient hub for bridleways
Which trace the flanks of fells,
Rosthwaite now lies dormant,
Couchant, settled in its ways,
A place where wreathes
Of woodsmoke winding upwards
Conjure cosy comfort and a log fire.

UP A ROCK LADDER

TO A

HANGING VALLEY AND MOUNTAIN TOP

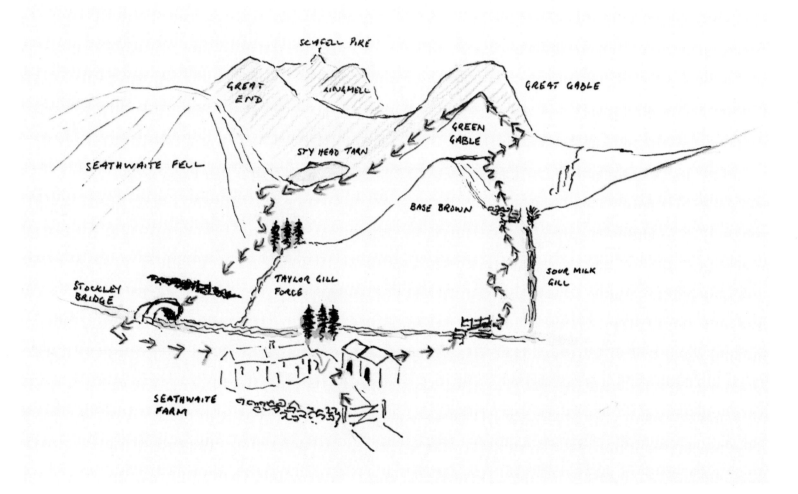

SCAFELL PIKE

GREAT END

LINGMELL

GREAT GABLE

GREEN GABLE

SPY HEAD TARN

SEATHWAITE FELL

BASE BROWN

STOCKLEY BRIDGE

TAYLOR GILL FORCE

SOUR MILK GILL

SEATHWAITE FARM

26

UP A ROCK LADDER TO A HANGING VALLEY AND MOUNTAIN TOP

This is a walk in rough country, including 2,250 feet of ascent and descent. Walking boots and protective clothing are essential and crampons desirable in winter conditions.

Seathwaite Farm is the starting point for many walks into the mountainous terrain emanating from Scafell Pike. To reach the farm take the Borrowdale Road (B5289) from Keswick and as the road begins to climb towards Honister Pass, just before Seatoller, turn left for Seathwaite. This is a quiet road used only by walkers, campers and local farmers. As soon as you see cars parked at the side of the road, start to look for a parking space which, during busy times of the year, is at a premium. Leave the car and continue along the road towards the farm. Go through the gate into the yard. Between byres on the right hand side, you will find an archway leading through the buildings to a walled track, take this and head towards a wooden footbridge over the River Derwent.

As you walk you may be able to see the workings of the old plumbago mines on the fell side across to the right. Plumbago was used in the making of pencils and gave rise to the Derwent Lakeland Pencil Factory which still exists in Keswick. The mines have long since been out of operation and today, plumbago is imported from the Far East. In Autumn, you may hear the sounds of shepherds calling and barks from their dogs as they bring their sheep down from the fells for the winter. They tumble over rocks like an avalanche.

Cross the footbridge, staying close to the stream and follow the track uphill beside the waterfalls known as Sour Milk Gill. A sloping ladder stile takes the path over a wall beside a rowan tree which seems to grow from rock. Height is quickly gained and views open up across to the fell on the other side of the valley, Glaramara, and down Borrowdale to Rosthwaite. Bright sunlight glints from the river changing it to molten gold. In Autumn, birch leaves fall in a spindrift, filling cups and chalices in rock with burnished copper. Seathwaite farm recedes to the size of a model with its sheep pens laid out below. The terrain is steep but interesting, with glimpses of the falls and attractive green pools appearing through trees on the right. At one point the path leaves the Gill and veers left.

Smooth slabs of rock rise on the right hand side of the path. This section can be dangerously icy during winter conditions, but otherwise is perfectly safe. Pass through a gate and return to the rocks beside the falls. Now it is necessary to scramble up a rocky stairway. At all times the path is enclosed and is not dangerous. The rushing water of the falls is a constant companion and there are splendid views of the head of the gill from various perches and overhanging rocks. Silver birches cling to crevices and smooth grey rocks form pinnacles on the skyline. In winter, the whole of the waterfall can be frozen, creating spectacular effects. Rock climbers seize the opportunity to extend their skills and try ice climbing up the waterfall. The air rings to the sound of their voices and ice axes.

At the top of the gill, take one last look at the valley below before heading over marshy ground beside the stream. The way now enters Gillercomb, a hanging valley scooped out by glaciers during the ice age. Across to the right is Raven Crag or Gillercomb Buttress, as it is known to climbers. Above, is Grey Knotts leading on to Brandreth. Our way continues into the valley in the shadow of Base Brown on the left, the track gradually rising until a steep section culminates in a saddle between Base Brown and Green Gable. Below lies Sty Head Pass, a bridleway linking Borrowdale with Wasdale and the still waters of Sty Head Tarn. This area featured in the novel Rogue Herries, by Hugh Walpole. Beyond Sty Head, rise the crags of Great End, leading to Ill Crag, Broad Crag and the notch of Scafell Pike. Almost separate is the conical outline of Lingmell. To the right rise the steep crags of Great Gable. On the distant horizon to the left, is a blue finger of rock Harrison Stickle over in Langdale.

Now turn right up the shoulder of the fell, following a cairned route towards the skyline. When you have reached the ridge, turn left and head upwards to the summit of Green Gable, 2,603 feet. Views of two other valleys now open up and you may look down into Buttermere and Ennerdale. Towering over Ennerdale are the blue shadowed flanks of Pillar with Pillar Rock, a favourite rock climb, showing as a notch on its flowing shoulder. Ahead, the view is dominated by the frowning rock of Gable Crag, and the solid hump of Gable itself. Between, lies a depression of 500 feet, aptly named Windy Gap, a graceful saddle between the two mountains. Continue with care down this track to the bottom of the saddle.

(Continued on page 29)

Seathwaite Farm

Seathwaite Farm is a last bastion of
domesticity.
Around, wild fells rear upwards
like vast fortress walls
Protecting lofty turrets of Scafell Pike
Great End, Great Gable.
A constant procession of assailants
wends its way
Across a yard ayelp with Border Collies.
Cobbles ground smooth by countless
boots
Shine like aluminium in weak winter
sunlight.
Patient beasts move within a barn
Made private by dark shadows.
Air moist and acrid hangs heavy
Yet holding familiarity within its
warmth.

Sour Milk Gill

In severe winters,
The gulley is strangely silent.
As a camera catches a fleeting moment,
So ice takes each droplet of water,
Retaining its movement,
Encapsulating the fall.
Ice blossoms in great chrysanthemum heads.
Intense cold, a living being,
Creeps stealthily up and around.
Dry rocks become friendly footholds,
While ice polishes each precipice.

Sty Head Tarn

The steep flanks of Aaron Slack
Stride downwards like great thighs
Beneath our feet, glinting like
a silver dollar
Sty Head Tarn lies waiting for us
to stoop
And pluck her from its icy wastes
And hold her tight - for luck.

Sprinkling Tarn

In winter, Sprinkling Tarn is paved with slabs of ice.
Great rents reveal water black and cold beneath.
Mist rises silently from Sty Head, like some evil genie.
It fleetingly touches Great End, then snakes upwards
To be lost against a grey sky.
A stone's fall echoes an instant, and then dies.
It is a place on the edge of eternity,
Where visitors are trespassers.

From here, the main track continues uphill to the summit of Great Gable. If you have sufficient time and energy you could go on to the summit, otherwise, at the bottom of Windy Gap, look for a path leading to the left and downwards over grass, indistinct at first and then becoming clear, as a stony, steeply descending track. This is named Aaron Slack an old name meaning scree - and as the path drops, so there is respite from the wind which rages over Windy Gap, the flanks of Gable and Green Gable affording welcome shelter. Your need to choose safe footholds amongst the stones will soon cause you to become intimately acquainted with their shapes and colour. They form an amazing palette of blue, grey, purple, green and ochre. Soon you will be walking in the company of a stream which gurgles deep beneath stones in the gully.

Eventually, Sty Head Tarn can be seen once more and above it, set below Great End, the waters of Sprinkling Tarn. The descent will probably bring the onset of 'jelly knees' but a level section from the tarn will restore their equilibrium. When the Tarn is reached, turn left along a track which follows the stream. This is the old bridleway from Seathwaite to Wasdale. Today it is an easy access route to many high fells and, as such, is frequently used by walkers and climbers. If you have time and would like to visit Sprinkling Tarn, turn right round the edge of the tarn until a major junction is reached. Bear left here heading uphill towards Great End. Sprinkling Tarn will be found at the foot of steep crags.

To return to our main route, after turning left at the foot of Aaron Slack, the track starts to descend, making its way in a series of zig zags down beside the cataract of Taylor Gill Force. Graceful larch trees hang over the path which runs beside a deep ravine. There is the constant silver whisper of a waterfall within its dark depths. Evening sunlight illuminates fronds of larch. Another track comes in from the right, heading down from Grains Gill and the two converge, going through a gate in a wall and over Stockley Bridge. Beneath, water tumbles in white torrents, smoothing grey boulders and rattling over loose stones.

(Continues on page 31)

Stockley Bridge arches gracefully over Grains Gill where white bubbling water pushes downwards over a jumble of stones. It stands at the junction of two major access routes to other Lakeland valleys used by dalesmen over the centuries. One track leads up beside Taylor Gill Force to Sty Head Tarn and over into Wasdale. The other climbs beside Grains Gill to Esk Hause then down Rosset Gill into Langdale. These ancient bridleways give quick access to the high fells enabling walkers to reach Scafell Pike, Great Gable, Bowfell and Great End, an area of exciting mountain terrain.

Look back and admire Taylor Gill Force in all its splendour, capturing the last rays of light, fringed in Autumn by dappled foliage of silver birch and larch. Now follow the path turning left after the beck, heading back to Seathwaite Farm.

If you're lucky, a small tea shop at the farm may be open and you will be able to enjoy some well earned refreshments. You have explored hanging valleys and ancient bridleways in the high fells.

DISCOVERING THE DELIGHTS

OF A

WILD AND LONELY VALLEY

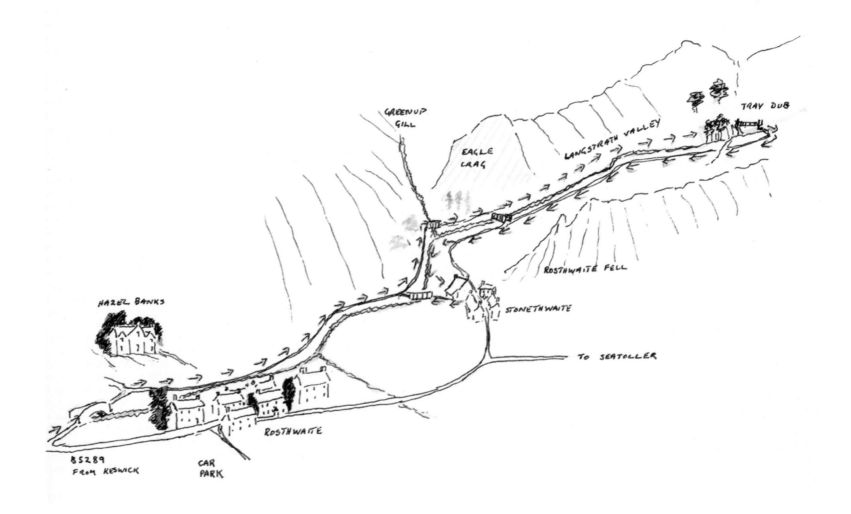

GREENUP GILL

EAGLE CRAG

LANGSTRATH VALLEY

TRAY DUB

ROSTHWAITE FELL

STONETHWAITE

HAZEL BANKS

TO SEATOLLER

ROSTHWAITE

B5289 FROM KESWICK

CAR PARK

DISCOVERING THE DELIGHTS OF A WILD AND LONELY VALLEY

Many field paths and bridleways lead into the fells from Rosthwaite. They connect villages and hamlets and before the existence of any road network, were used by shepherds and quarry men to move stock and goods from one dale to another. Today these rights of way are used largely by fell walkers as quick access to the high places. One such track follows Langstrath Beck.

The way begins on the Borrowdale road at Rosthwaite. Driving from Keswick to Rosthwaite, turn right opposite the shop and park beside the Village Hall. Retrace your steps to the main road and turn left opposite the shop turning right almost immediately. Go over the bridge towards Hazel Bank and then turn right heading for Stonethwaite. A stony lane between dry stone walls follows Stonethwaite Beck. Across the water is the rear of the Royal Oak Hotel and the back bar of the Scafell Hotel. Soon the path bends left, and a beautiful sweep of calm river appears. On a clear day its waters are a brilliant blue. Beyond are the fields and hamlets of Borrowdale. A slate slab bridges a runnel of water and on what is almost an exclusive miniature island there is a stone bench, an ideal place to sit and admire the view.

The track leads on, leaving the river, with a stone wall on the right and fellside with open woodland on the left. Take a moment to examine the stone walls and enjoy the brilliantly coloured lichens, many small ferns, stone crops and mosses growing in their crevices. Admire too, the skill and patience of those who built the walls; two together with a filling of rubble and through stones linking and strengthening them. You may find your steps are made in the company of Herdwick sheep and sometimes working dogs and shepherds. Herdwicks are quite a distinctive breed. They have a short, wiry, bilberry coloured fleece and white face which usually has a contented expression. They are adept at surviving in the rugged, bleak conditions of a Lakeland winter and there are many apocryphal stories about their homing instincts. Along this stretch of path it is common to find Herdwicks sheltering in a bend in the wall.

Across the river and fields, the white houses of Stonethwaite come into view. A walled lane from Stonethwaite joins the path here. There are many places in the Lake District which end in thwaite, a word of Norse origin meaning a stony place, in a wild area, cleared for cultivation. This is certainly true of Stonethwaite for the fells and fields hereabouts are littered with boulders and stones fallen from the surrounding high peaks. If you wish to join the path at Stonethwaite, park beside the post box on the left of the road just as it enters the village and take the lane to the left of the post box signposted Greenup and Grasmere. At the end of the lane turn right.

Now the crags of Rosthwaite Fell or Bessyboot, as it is affectionately known, tower above Stonethwaite. Ahead, Eagle Crag guards the entrance to two converging valleys, Langstrath and Greenup. Rising steeply through the woods on the left is a path taking walkers up to Dock Tarn and Ullscarf. In summer, the rough pastureland is studded with flowers; coltsfoot, harebells, thyme and meadow sweet. Their fragrance wafts pleasantly on the air. Spires of purple foxgloves border the path. Luxuriant bracken on the fellside turns tawny gold in Autumn, while trees of mixed woodland clothing rising rocky platforms, are ablaze with reds and golds.

Continue to follow the path; sometimes it splits into two, creating an upper and lower track and there are a number of streams to cross as they busily find their way down to the main watershed. After heavy rain you may find you have to pick your way through flooded areas. Soon, as you cross a bridge, the wall is replaced by a wire fence and a view of the beck opens up. During a sudden downpour up on the fells, streams and rivers can rapidly change from quiet meandering strands to raging torrents. Here, the beck rushes between grassy banks in a foaming mass of activity and there is the constant chatter of water over stones. The path rises steadily, passing a ruined barn, always overshadowed by Eagle Crag, its visage changing with constantly shifting light. Below, the River Derwent scoops smooth chalices from silver grey rock, its jade waters glistening in steely light, casting back blades of light like sharp crystals. Cataracts of stones debouch from the high fells, torn down by previous storms and action of ancient glaciers. A boarded walkway eases the path over all this upheaval. Soon, a bridge over the beck comes into view.

Here, at the foot of Eagle Crag, Langstrath and Greenup Valleys converge. The path ahead continues to climb beside Greenup Gill, resolutely heading for Grasmere, but leave this to be explored on another day and turn right

(Continues on page 37)

Stonethwaite

Farmsteads in Stonethwaite sit at the foot of Bessyboot,
Like Grandfather in his Queen Anne chair,
Waiting for winter to pass.
Above them, air impregnated with peat
Sweeps across Ullscarf's undulating folds
And Eagle Crag pushes its nose upwards
To scent snow on distant Helvellyn.

through the gate, taking the path which goes towards a footbridge crossing Greenup Gill. An inscription on the bridge is a memorial to a young member of Manchester mountaineering club, who died of exhaustion in this valley in 1939, a reminder to walkers of their own fallibility in this rugged environment and the need to give just regard to its inherent dangers. Just beyond the bridge you will find a waters meet, where Langstrath Beck and Greenup Gill converge. A delightful spot. Here cascades tumble between crevices falling into clear green pools. A place to linger and possibly picnic. After admiring the falls, return to the path with Eagle Crag to your left. Since the way ahead continues over marshy ground it is sometimes easier to walk over the sloping boulders of the stream bed. Soon a group of stately larch trees drape their elegant fronds over the rushing torrent and there are further falls to admire. After a short while the stream banks are clothed in birch woodland. A little wicket gate opens onto a wooden bridge leading to a lane which returns to Stonethwaite. If you wish to shorten the walk, cross over the bridge and turn right towards the village. When the wall on the right ends you will find a stile leading into fields beside the beck. Go over this and explore the stream path on your return to Stonethwaite. (See directions at the end of this description)

If you would like a longer walk, the path continues beyond the bridge, climbing and winding, undulating over rough and stony ground towards the head of the valley and the blue silhouette of Esk Pike. This is wild country with no habitation or shelter. Soon, the horizon is dominated on the left by an upstanding rock, a boulder deposited by a glacier during the ice age. It appears like a castle from the banks of the Rhine. Clouds above gather and swell, bourne on by air currents rising up the steep cliff faces. Beneath your feet the rock blooms into rose red porphyria, a substance used to carve Napoleon's coffin. Look out too, for lines of white quartz, wandering like snails' tracks over the face of rock. The path winds round the base of the boulder and heads towards a ladder stile. Don't go over this just yet but turn right and head over the grass towards a thundering sound. Below the path, Langstrath Beck picks its way through stones, marsh and gravel, changing its course according to its whim. Narrow channels worn into a rock bed, have created places where shepherds have gathered their flocks together for shearing and dipping. This is Blackmoss Pot.

(Continued on page 39)

Blackmoss Pot is one of several deep pools in Langstrath Beck. Here water rushes through a narrow cleft between two rock faces, seething and swirling many feet below. Shepherds use these pools for washing sheep before gathering them in nearby folds to shear them.

Here, deep water is forced between narrow sheer rock walls, foaming and seething as it passes this natural barrier. It is a good place to picnic, for shelter can often be found amongst its rocky outcrops but explore with care.

Return to the ladder stile. Go over and continue up the valley. The path passes another rocky bluff on the left and then winds on, close to the beck which at this point is wide and stony. The crags on the right lead upwards to Glaramara, 2,000 feet above. Now the skyline at the head of the valley changes and Esk Pike is replaced by Bowfell.
Old stunted rowan or mountain ash trees, are dotted over the fellside. On the left, water drains from the flanks of Rosset Pike creating Stake Beck, crossed by a footbridge. Just before the bridge turn right and head down towards Langstrath Beck and another footbridge over Tray Dub.

Here is another narrow channel with water rushing below into deep green pools. Jade and pink wrinkled rocks rise from its surface. If the day is calm and there are no ripples on the surface, it is possible to look through the magnifying glass of water to glimpse those same bands of quartz in the bedrock beneath. Mountain ash and holly bushes grace the banks.

Now prepare to return to Stonethwaite via the other side of the valley and admire its wide sweep created by glaciers during the ice age. This path never gives up its travellers without whipping the senses into some kind of response. On more than one occasion we have hurried as fast as the stones would allow to keep ahead of an approaching storm, only to be drenched to the skin before reaching Stonethwaite. On other occasions, returning from the high fells, Langstrath has earned its title and every stone of the long track back has been sorely felt. On those rare fine and sunny days, it's a delight to feel bare legs brushed with spikey phragmites reeds and scent the sweet smell of turf and herbage. But warm sun on the back, rain lashing and driving one onwards, black clouds gathering, wind tearing and raging, all the elements only add to this remote valley's captivating appeal.

(Continued on page 42)

One of the delights to be discovered when exploring the Langstrath Valley is Tray Dub where the beck is forced through a narrow rocky channel. This is the only safe crossing place after Stonethwaite.

I was intrigued by a number of twisted, gnarled old rowan or mountain ash trees growing over the fellside at the head of Langstrath near Tray Dub. This one appeared to have been burnt. I wondered if it might have been struck by lightning at some time. It had a hole in its trunk which might provide a good shelter for some wild animal. The outer layer of the trunk of the rowan is soft but the heartwood is extremely tough and was used for making wooden farm implements. Rowan is the Scottish name derived from the Gaelic rudha-an meaning the red one, referring to its brilliant red Autumn berries. It is a small tree growing to about 30 feet and is usually 'planted' by birds who drop the seeds from its berries. They grow in some unlikely crevices and cracks in the rock. In Scotland, it was often planted near farms as a safeguard against witchcraft.

The return path, beneath Glaramara, is straightforward. A large slab of pink and grey rock slopes across the path at one point but there are grooves and footholds so it presents no problems. Soon, where the wall comes down from the fell on both sides of the valley, you are back at Black Moss Pot. Afterwards the path rises and the trees at the waters meet come into view. The path leads back to the gated bridge. Do not cross the bridge. Follow the path straight ahead beneath ancient birch and oak trees, enjoying glimpses of the river as you go. The track leads downhill beneath soft fronds of larch trees with views of the falls polishing slabs of rock. Sturdy oak branches reach out to touch the water. A large blue-grey boulder perched on end, stands on the right hand side of the path. At this point, bear right, away from the main path and go down to a lovely stretch of river. This is a place to linger and enjoy the sight and sound of waterfalls cascading into green pools shaded by overhanging oak trees. Cross over the stile and continue your exploration of the river bank. Green rocks shelve down below the water's surface. On fine days, all is overlaid with brilliant blue from a reflected sky. Climb the rocky bank now towards a ladder stile and cross over into a campsite. Go through a gate and cross a field. Soon the houses of Stonethwaite lie ahead. Go through a gate onto the road beside the Langstrath Hotel. Here you can partake of refreshments. To return, continue along the road through Stonethwaite village, until, at a bend, you see a telephone box beside a lane marked Greenup Gill and Grasmere. Go down the lane across the bridge and turn left to retrace your steps to Rosthwaite. *The Royal Oak serves tea and scones from 3:45 to 5 p.m. and during the winter you can relax in front of a log fire.

You have explored a wildly beautiful valley, sculpted over the years by water and ice.

* The Royal Oak is closed during December

Langstrath Beck
Loveliest of rivers,
When God created you,
He put all that was beautiful here;
Swift gossiping shallows
Tossing about the rumours of stones,
Deep, silent, green pools - waiting,
Steep cliffs frowning down,
Reclining boulders - bilberry blue,
Bold brown branches, dipping low,
When God created rivers -
This was you.